B. Ludy

introducing
quilting

introducing quilting

Eirian Short

Charles Scribner's Sons
New York

Printed in Great Britain
Library of Congress Catalog Card Number 73-14038
SBN 684-13652-X (cloth)

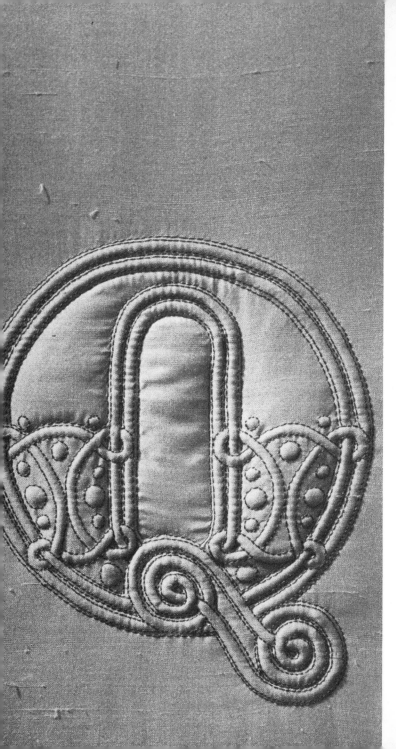

contents

Acknowledgment

I should like to thank The Embroiderers' Guild for permission to reproduce figure 57; the Victoria and Albert Museum for figures 5 and 34; and Miss Averil Colby and Mrs Nigel Morgan for figure 26.

As usual, principals of colleges have allowed students' work to be used, and heads of departments have been most helpful in sending me work to photograph or in arranging photographic sessions themselves. For this I am grateful. Thanks go to Mr G Cunliffe at the College of All Saints for permission to use figure 37; to Mr Derrick Turner and Miss June Tiley at Cardiff College of Art for students' work in figures 16, 78, 79, 88, 91, 92 and colour plate 3; to Mr Michael Pattrick and Miss Colleen Farr at the Central School of Art and Design for figure 84; to Mr Jon Thompson and Miss Constance Howard of the Faculty of Fine Art at Goldsmiths' College for figures 3, 8, 10, 17, 18, 38, 47, 48, 49, 50, 51, 52, 56, 58, 60, 62, 63, 86 and colour plates 4 and 5; to Mr H H Shelton and Mrs Nouche Thomas at the Faculty of Art and Design, Middlesex Polytechnic for figures 76, 77 and colour plates 2, 8 and 9; to Mr A Saunders and Mr Roger Limbrick at the London College of Furniture for figure 93 and colour plate 6; and to Mr R E R Downing and Miss Anne Butler of the Embroidery School, Faculty of Art and Design, Manchester Polytechnic for figures 15, 21, 22, 23, 24, 81 and 87.

I am also grateful to Mrs Anne Preston, Mrs Eve Lindsay and Mrs Barbara Siedlecka for lending me examples of their work, and to Miss Maureen Whyberd for a page from her design notebook.

Lastly, my thanks go to my husband, Denys Short, who was at all times willing to leave his own work to help me, in particular by taking all but a few of the photographs in the book.

introduction

Quilting consists of two or more layers of fabric stitched through by hand or machine, to form a decorative surface pattern. It falls into several distinct categories, often referred to by geographical labels such as 'English' and 'Italian' which are quite unjustified. As quilting is common to nearly all countries and was practised long before England or Italy existed as such, I have adopted the method advocated by Averil Colby in her book *Quilting* and classified each type of quilting by the technique used rather than by the supposed place of origin. Under this system the four main categories are as follows.

wadded quilting

(also known as 'English' and 'American' quilting)
This is the oldest form of quilting, based on the securing together of several layers of material to provide protection against cold and discomfort. Wadded quilting consists of a top fabric and backing between which is sandwiched a filling of whatever thickness is required, depending on what the end product is to be. These are some suggestions for its application:

On dress For extra warmth in housecoats, waistcoats, coat linings, dressing jackets, windcheaters, slippers; for added weight round hems of skirts and evening coats; as decorative detailing on otherwise plain garments, in the form of cuffs, collars, revers or pockets; as accessories in the form of hats, caps, belts, bags, etc.

In the home For extra warmth as bedcovers, draughtproof curtains, teapot or coffeepot covers; for added comfort on hard benches, unupholstered chairs and on bedheads; as interesting textural decoration on cushions, pillows, mirror frames, jewel boxes, work boxes, etc.

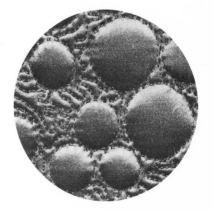

flat quilting

This has no padding but is merely stitching taken through two layers of fabric. Apart from its value as decoration, its main function is, in dress, to give added weight to a flimsy fabric, and harder wearing qualities at points of friction such as cuffs, collars and pockets; and, in the home, on large articles such as bedcovers and curtains, to strengthen and enliven big, plain areas of 'background' between scattered embroidered motifs.

corded quilting

(also known as 'Italian' quilting)
Used in an open linear design, corded quilting fulfils much the same function as flat quilting, but if whole areas are corded solidly the resulting quality is more like that of wadded quilting. In this form it can be used in conjunction with stuffed quilting or embroidered motifs to form the entire background to a bed quilt, combining warmth and weight with a rich texture. All corded quilting designs are based on parallel pairs of lines which are stitched through two fabrics to form channels, through which the cord is threaded to make a raised pattern.

stuffed quilting

(also known as Trapunto)
Stuffed quilting, like corded quilting, is padded after the stitching is complete, making it particularly suitable for carrying out large projects on the machine, when wadded quilting becomes unmanageable. It consists of enclosed shapes padded from behind to stand out in high relief on the right side of the work. Its main application is as a decoration, but, like corded quilting, if massed together it will take on some of the qualities of wadded quilting. Different types of quilting may be put together in various combinations. For instance, on a design in wadded quilting, certain focal points could be emphasised by additional stuffing. Alternatively, stuffed and corded quilting may be combined to give a balanced mixture of solid and linear elements in a design.

right and overleaf
1   Suggestions for the use of quilting
on clothes   Maureen Whyberd

10

Any of the above techniques when worked on transparent fabrics are known as 'Shadow Quilting' and, when coloured fillings which show through the top fabric are used, an added interest is given to the work.

Quilting can be combined with other forms of embroidery such as surface stitchery, beading, appliqué etc. Whether these are worked before or after the quilting process will depend on individual cases, though generally speaking, appliqué would be worked before quilting, beading afterwards, etc. Also included in the book

2 *Riding the waves* Eirian Short

are some techniques which, without being true quilting, are closely enough related to it to merit inclusion. Some, for instance tied and gathered quilting, are offshoots of traditional methods; others, such as pillow quilting, are modern, time-saving short cuts. One method does away with stitching altogether, making use of an iron on interlining to bond the layers together. This is, of course, more limited in its application as it would not stand up to the laundering or dry cleaning necessary for garments or soft furnishings. It has

3 *right* Panel combining quilting and surface stitchery   Marion Gilling

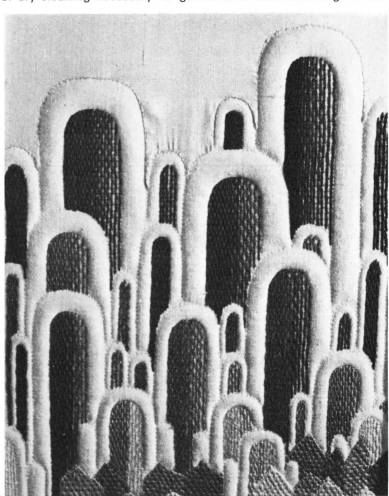

Plate 1 *opposite* *The Round Pond.* Quilted swan with painting, fabric collage and found objects. One of a series of swan panels by Eirian Short.

a part to play, however, in the use of quilted effects in 'fine art' works executed in fabric. In this field, the tendency over the last few years has been for a greater three-dimentional quality, and in present day exhibitions of embroidery and fabric collage panels, padding and quilting techniques are much in evidence. Quilting has also been used by some American artists who normally work in paint or print, furthering the present tendency to break down the barriers between one art form and another.

4   *below*   Heraldic Swan making a wall decoration in a bathroom. The use of PVC which can be sponged down makes the large areas of white practicable   Eirian Short

5   *overleaf*   Section of man's cap, (18th century) showing quilting and pulled work combined   Victoria and Albert Museum, Crown copyright

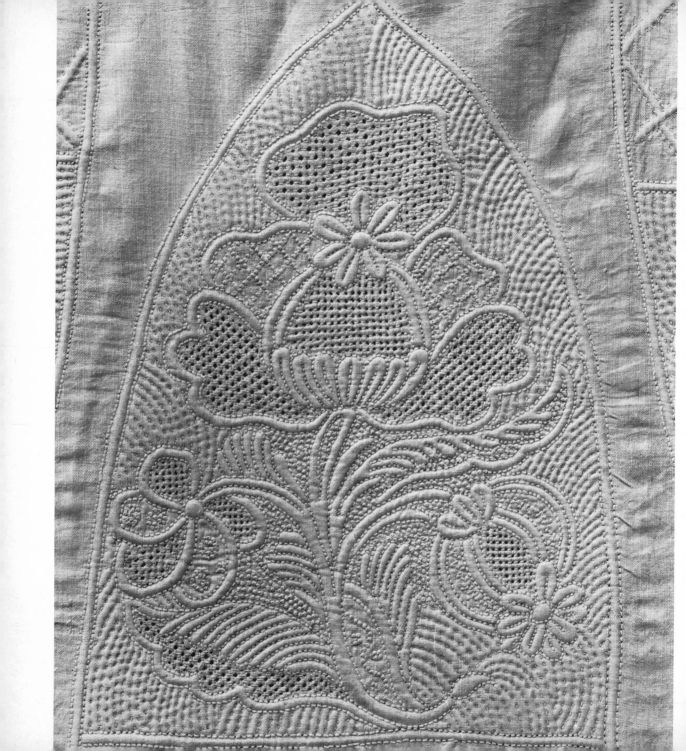

wadded quilting

(also known as 'English' Quilting)

construction   Three layers – top fabric, filling and backing held together by all over stitching (figure 6).

purpose   To give extra warmth; to cushion against hardness; to enliven surface texture.

materials   *Top fabric*   any smooth, closely woven fabric such as cotton, fine linen, silk; light leather, suède, chamois. Materials made from man-made fibres do not quilt as well as natural ones, being too springy. Light tones show up the quilting more effectively than dark ones; matt or shiny surfaces are a matter of personal preference.
Filling   for slight padding use fluffy domette (a loosely knitted cotton fabric); one layer or more of a soft fabric such as flannel or foam-backed jersey (this is good because it does not move about during the quilting process).
For greater padding use synthetic wadding, which comes in several thicknesses.
Backing   when the backing will be seen (as in a bed cover) use the same material as top fabric, or a cheaper version of it. When the backing is hidden (as in a lined garment) use quilting muslin, butter muslin (cheesecloth), organdie or mull.

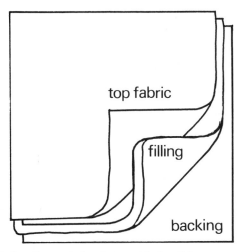

top fabric

filling

backing

6   Construction for wadded quilting: top fabric, filling and backing

threads   Match to top fabric, ie silk on silk, cotton on cotton. On cotton use a 40 or 50 cotton or buttonhole twist. The colour should match the top fabric, but can be in a darker tone.

15

7 *above* Non-repeating all-over pattern from natural source (magnified cross section of lichen)

stitches *By hand* running stitch, back stitch, chain stitch, pearl (figure 85).
By machine straight stitching, satin stitch, automatic stitches or free running.
The stitching should be distributed over the whole surface of the work in order to hold the three layers of material together. This can be done in

(a) An all over repeating pattern Take a basic motif or unit and repeat it in one of a number of possible formal arrangements. The motif can be geometric (square, circle, hexagon, etc) or 'organic' (pebble, leaf, shell, etc) or based on a man-made object (cogwheel, bottle, wrought iron, etc). Simplest repeat of all is the stripe, which can be used in varying widths, straight or curved. A square and a shell are shown in a variety of repeats in figure 13 and figure 14.

(b) An all over pattern which does not repeat Many such patterns are found in nature and can be adapted for quilting (figure 7); others can be developed by chance effects such as dribbling paint, taking rubbings from textured surfaces, etc.

(c) A design planned to fill a specific shape This might take the form, for instance, of a pictorial motif (figure 15) or an arrangement of centrepiece and borders as found on traditional country quilts (figures 16 and 26).

designs Designs for the machine should be kept simple unless the machinist is experienced enough to work free running, by removing the foot on the machine. This is not recommended for beginners.

method 1 Iron top fabric and backing.
2 Mark on design if paint or crayon is being used. Other, less permanent methods of marking are best left until later (see page 74).
3 Tack all layers together, thoroughly smoothing the fabrics while sewing. For small pieces tack out from centre; for larger ones, in a horizontal and vertical grid (see page 73).

If the work is being framed for quilting stretch backing on frame, smooth out filling and top fabric and tack through all three on frame. If a frame is not being used spread out layers on a table or on the floor. Never skimp on the tacking, as adequate tacking will prevent 'riding' of the materials during work.
4 Mark designs which are to be chalked or needlemarked. Only mark as much as you can work at one sitting as this type of marking

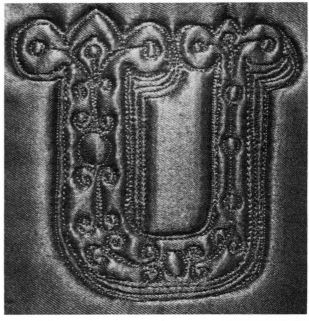

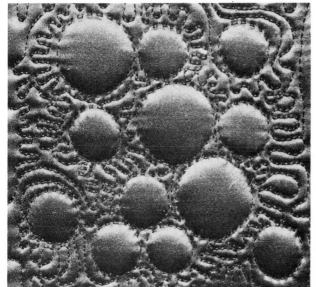

8 *above left* Motif in wadded quilting worked by hand in running stitch Sue Jenner

9 *above right* Initial letter U worked in free running on the sewing machine

10 *left* Wadded quilting, hand stitched in back stitch. Note how the plain areas stand out in strong relief from the closely quilted background Ingrid Rowling

rubs off with handling. When machining simple geometric repeats it is often enough to mark only the first line in any direction (see figure 11).

5   Carry out stitching by hand or machine.

6   Remove tacking.

7   Finish in one of the ways shown in figure 19. Remember that the work will 'shrink' during the quilting process, so always allow for this when cutting out materials.

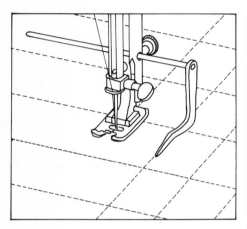

11   Using the gauge or edge marker to space out lines of stitching

12   *right*   Stuffed, corded, wadded and tied quilting combined

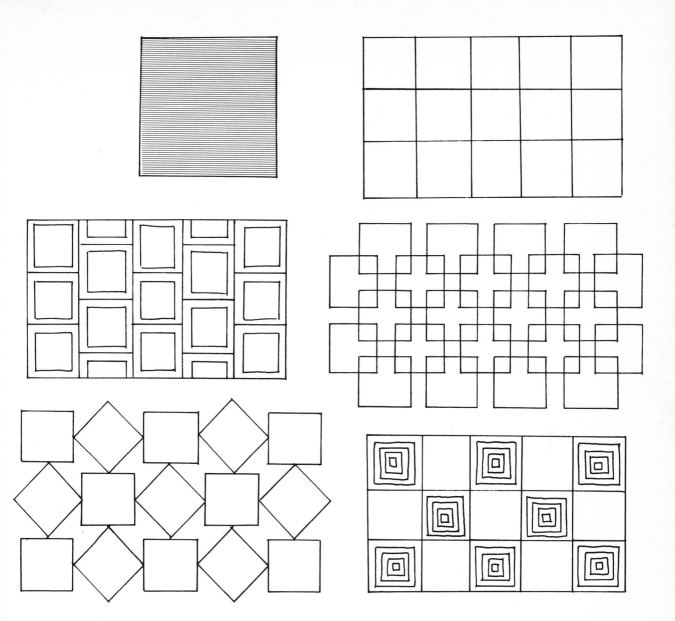

13   Square template used to build up
all-over repeating patterns

14 *below* Designs based on the shell template

15 *opposite* Panel Pat Hopcraft

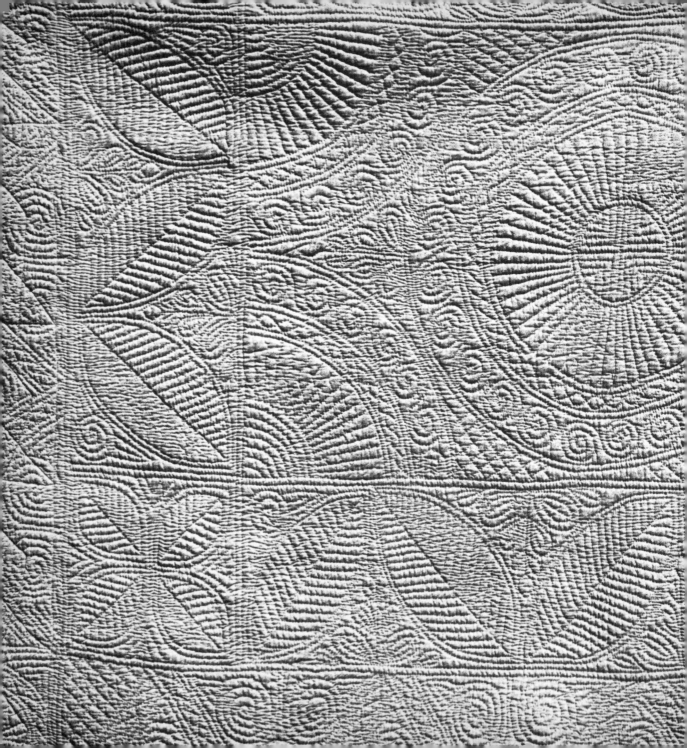

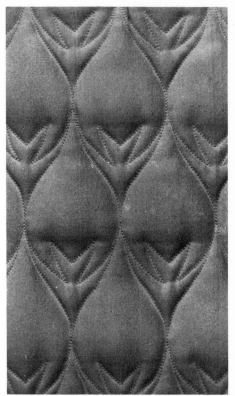

17, 18 Two experimental pieces. The overall repeating pattern worked by Sister Helen McGing, *above*, and the highly padded design by Ingrid Rowling, *left*, have both been stitched on the machine and afterwards sprayed. The spraying, in a dye of a darker tone than the ground fabric, gives an added intensity to the shadow

16 *opposite* Detail of Welsh quilt, circa 1890

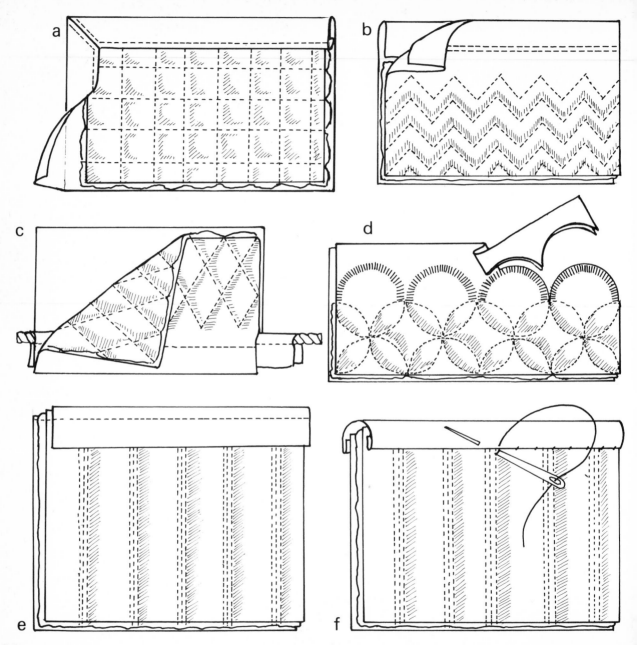

19 *opposite* Finishes for wadded quilting
(a)   Bringing the backing over on to the front of the work and machining it down
(b)   Turning in the top fabric and backing and machining them together
(c)   Inserting a piping cord between backing and top fabric
(d) Working scallops and trimming away surplus material
(e) and (f)   Binding

20   *left*   Gingham tucked, pleated and quilted   Anne Preston

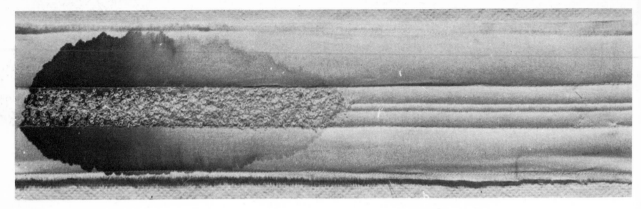

21, 22 *above and opposite above*
Two roughs from a series produced by
experimenting with mixed techniques.
Colour has been flooded on to the
fabric with *Procion* dyes, and quilting
and embroidery worked on the machine.
One piece includes an applied strip of
machine knitting   Karen Nicol

23, 24 *right and opposite below*
Design for a bed quilt. The detail shows
part of the design carried out in Fine
Art Transfer Crayons, with machine
quilting   Anita Eastwood

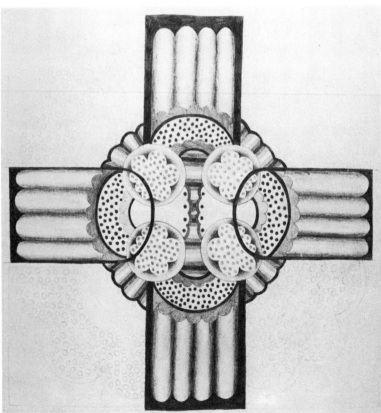

25 Appliqué and quilting carried out in one operation using satin stitch on the machine

26 *overleaf* Welsh quilt, lined with 19th century cotton print. Said to have been made 1770

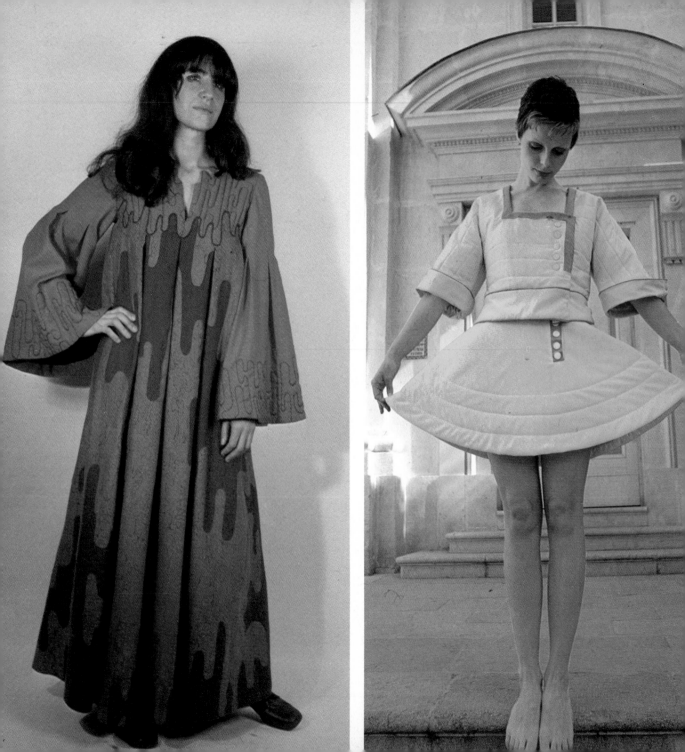

tied quilting

Wadded quilting can be tied instead of stitched. The work is prepared as for ordinary wadded quilting, but must be framed. Instead of the layers being joined with lines of stitching they are secured at spaced-out points by a knot. Use a strong thread – buttonhole twist, cotton a broder, pearl cotton or a linen thread would be suitable.

method Tack layers of fabric together in a frame. Bring thread through fabric from the back leaving an end of about 50 mm (2 in.). Work two small stitches on the same spot, taking the end through to back of work and tying it with the end already there with two or three firm knots (figure 28). Trim off ends close to knot.

variations A bead or button can be attached while making the second small stitch (figure 29); or the tying can be done on the right side of the work, the ends being left slightly longer and tied into a small decorative bow.

27 Tied quilting
Left: knot only
Right: knot with bead

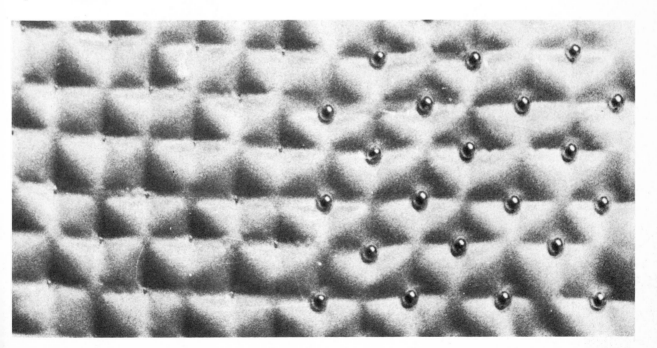

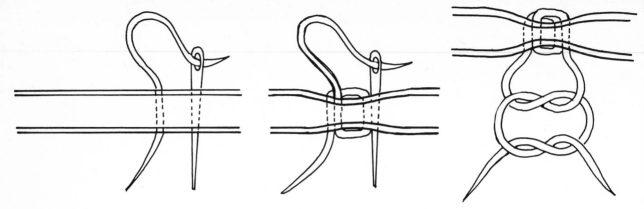

28   The knot for tied quilting

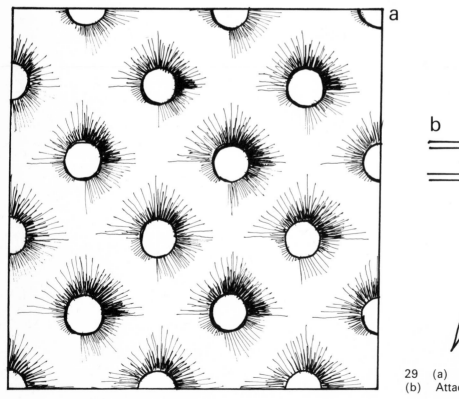

a

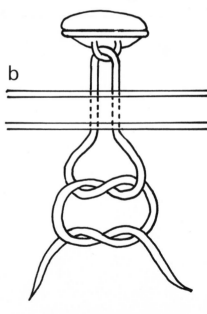

b

29   (a)   Tied quilting with buttons
      (b)   Attaching the button (or bead)

lap quilting

In most present-day homes a frame for setting up a bed quilt is too big to be practical, but large projects can nevertheless be undertaken by 'lap quilting', ie stitching the work in sections, putting the pieces together when the quilting is done. This method is also helpful with machine quilting as a double bed quilt is very cumbersome to manipulate on the machine.

construction   Blocks of wadded quilting joined together.

purpose   To carry out large projects in a confined space, or to facilitate handling on the machine.

materials   As for wadded quilting, allowing plenty for the extra seaming involved.

designs   The design must be planned to divide naturally into four, six or eight sections, or into strips. These are known as *blocks*.

method   Work each block as for ordinary wadded quilting, allowing ample material for turnings on top fabric and backing (figure 30a). When the quilting is completed trim the filler in each block to the exact size required, then lay two blocks face to face on each other and seam up the top fabric close to edge of filler (figure 30b); Open out (figure 30c). Repeat with two more blocks until the whole of the top is joined into one piece. Trim surplus material from seams. Turn over work and join up the backing. If the backing will be on view, as in a two sided quilt, this joining must be done neatly by turning in edges and slipstitching or oversewing them together (figure 30d). Tapes can be stitched over the seams to camouflage them and make an attractive criss cross pattern. The joins on the top side can be concealed by working one or two rows of quilting along them after the joining up is completed.

The waistcoat by Eve Lindsay (figure 31) was worked in eight pieces which were afterwards joined.

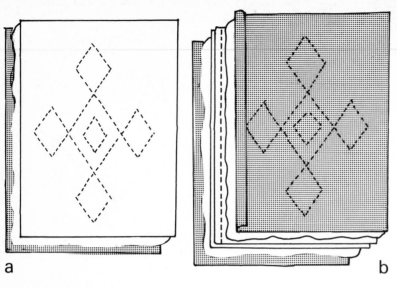

30   Lap quilting. Joining the completed blocks together
(a)   A completed block
(b)   Two blocks seamed together, face to face
(c)   The blocks opened out
(d)   The back neatened

31   *opposite*   Waistcoat quilted on silk. The waistcoat, which has a leather back, is worked in a combination of quilting techniques and some surface embroidery, and fastened with a hand-made cord   Eve Lindsay

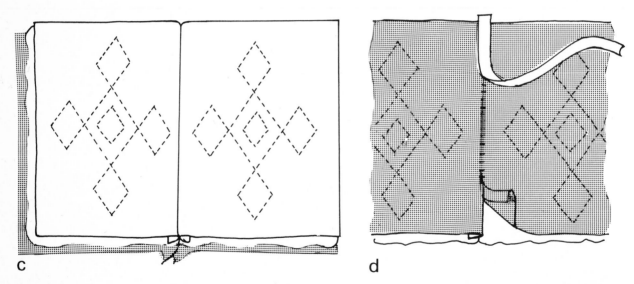

flat quilting

construction *Two layers* top fabric and backing, held together by all over stitching (figure 32).

purpose To add weight to a flimsy fabric; to give protection at a point of hard wear (eg on the cuffs or pockets of a garment); to give a little extra warmth, without bulk, or to enliven large plain areas of 'background' fabric between scattered embroidered motifs.

materials *Top fabric* any smooth closely woven fabric (as for wadded quilting).
Backing as top fabric, or cheaper version of the same; muslin, organdie, or, if greater stiffness is required, a non-woven inter-lining.

For a reversible garment two layers of foam backed fabric in contrasting colours could be used, back to back.

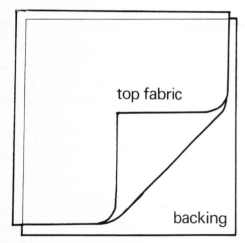

32   Construction for flat quilting: top fabric and backing

threads Match to top fabric (ie cotton on cotton, etc).

stitches *By hand* any line stitch (back, running, chain stem, etc).
By machine as there is little undulation in the fabric in flat quilting, straight machine stitching looks a little thin, so a satin

stitch, automatic embroidery stitch or cable stitch may be worked. (For cable stitch see page 82.)

designs Any fairly evenly distributed linear design.

method 1 Iron top fabric and backing.
2 Mark on design (see page 74).
3 Tack fabric and backing together, right sides outwards (see page 73).
4 Stitch by hand or machine.
5 Remove tackings.

33 *below* Flat quilting on an 18th century pillow cover   Victoria and Albert Museum, Crown copyright

34 *overleaf* Flat quilting using back stitches in varying lengths

corded quilting

(also known as 'Italian' quilting)

construction Two layers of fabric with cord insertion (figure 35).

purpose Mainly decoration, although the cording does add extra weight to a flimsy fabric. Sometimes in combination with stuffed quilting the background is solidly corded, giving real warmth and weight (figure 36).

materials *Top fabric*   any smooth, closely woven fabric, soft leather, suède, chamois and, handled with care, PVC.
Backing   butter muslin (cheesecloth), linen scrim or any soft, loosely woven fabric.
Insertion   cotton cord, such as piping cord or candlewick; rug wool; or, for softer effects, Italian quilting wool or knitting wool of appropriate thickness.

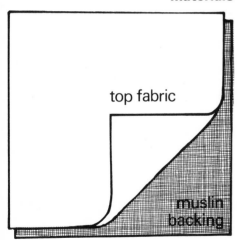

35   Construction for corded quilting:
top fabric with muslin backing

threads Match to top fabric (ie cotton on cotton, etc).

stitches Back stitch or straight machine stitching.

designs To facilitate working, designs should be built up from long continuous parallel lines. Interlacing borders and all over patterns from classical sources are particularly suitable and can be adapted to fit the required space (figure 39). Original designs can be planned by pinning string or piping cord on a piece of soft board, trying different arrangements of lines until a satisfactory design is achieved (figure 40).

method

1   Iron top fabric well.
2   Spread out backing and place top fabric, face uppermost on it. Tack together thoroughly (see page 73).
3   Transfer design to top fabric by any of the methods explained on page 74. Make sure all lines are double.
4   Carry out stitching by hand (back stitch) or machine (straight stitch).
5   Take out tacking.
6   Turn work over. Select thread which, when inserted, will comfortably fill the space between the parallel lines of stitching.

36   Stuffed motif standing out from a background of solid cording

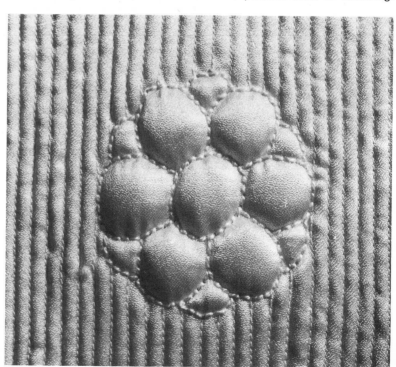

Thread into tapestry needle or rug needle (depending on its thickness).

Insert the needle into the backing, between two lines of stitching, making sure that the needle does not pierce the top fabric. Push needle along, drawing thread between lines. Whenever a strong curve or sharp angle in the line is reached bring the needle out and reinsert it at the same point, leaving a small amount of cord projecting each time (figure 41). This prevents the work 'cockling'. Where lines of cording cross bring the needle out on one side of the line to be crossed and insert it on the other side of the line.

Note if cotton cord is used for the filling it should be soaked in water first to shrink it, otherwise the first time the quilted article is washed distortion will occur. Dry it thoroughly before use.

7 Trim off all ends of cords to about 3 mm ($\frac{1}{8}$ in.). Corded quilting must be lined.

37 Simple geometric design in corded quilting on red PVC Ann Newman

38 *left* Corded quilting. Diagonal cording on striped fabric Sister Agnes Bernard

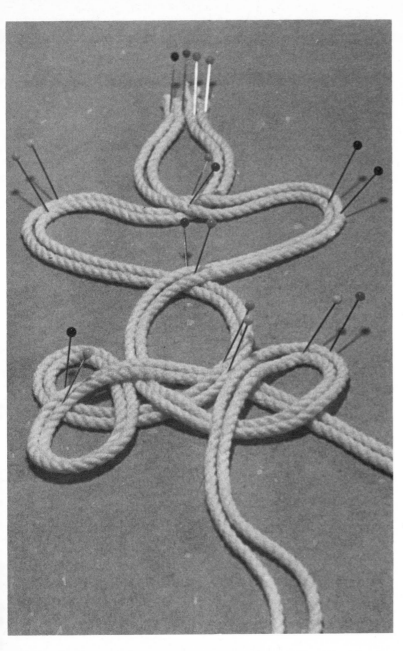

39 *opposite* Interlacing border designs from classical sources, suitable for corded quilting

40 *left* Planning a design for corded quilting by pinning piping cord on soft board

41 *below* Inserting the padding in corded quilting

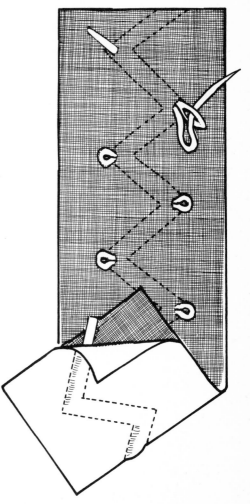

corded quilting in a single fabric

(a) By hand, on a single layer of fabric

The appearance of corded quilting can be achieved on a single fabric by securing a cord to the underside of the fabric with a double back stitch. Use a firm cord, holding it in position under the fabric with the left hand, while working the double back stitch with the right hand on the upper side of the fabric (figure 42). Alternatively, the design can be traced on the back of the work and the stitching done from the back in a close herringbone. The effect on the right side is identical but the second method requires greater care in execution to produce neat lines of backstitching on the right side (figure 43).

42 *above* Corded quilting on a single layer of fabric worked from the right side

43 *below* Cord attached to single layer of fabric working from the wrong side

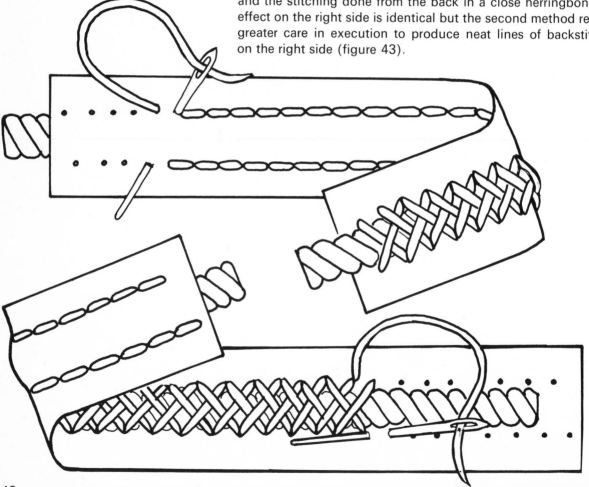

(b) By machine, with a raised seam attachment

Some sewing machines have an attachment which, used with a twin needle, produces a raised line very similar to corded quilting. This would only be suitable for simple designs (figure 44).

44　Using the raised seam attachment with twin needles

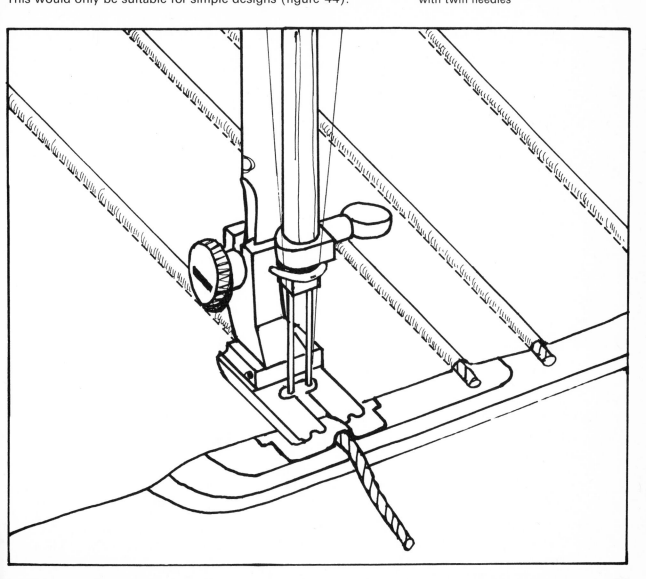

stuffed quilting

(also known as Trapunto)

construction *Two layers*   top fabric and backing with some areas padded (figure 45).

purpose To give weight; to emphasise parts of a design.

materials *Top fabric*   any smooth closely woven fabric, as for wadded and corded quilting.
Backing   loosely woven muslin or linen scrim.
Filling   wadding.

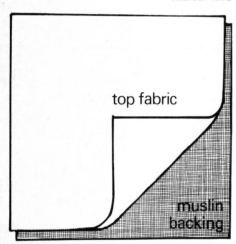

45   Construction for stuffed quilting:
top fabric and muslin backing

threads Match to top fabric (ie cotton on cotton, etc).

stitches *By hand*   back stitch.
By machine   free darning.

designs Designs must be built up from small enclosed units, which may be formal and geometric in character, or free shapes with a more organic feeling.

Small units may be grouped together to form a larger motif, doing away with any 'bitty' effect of the small shapes which go to make up the design.

Stuffed quilting combines well with corded quilting, the enclosed shapes making an interesting contrast with the linear quality of the cording (figure 48).

Stuffed motifs can be made to stand out from a background of solid cording, where weight and warmth are required as well as decoration (figure 36).

method

1   Iron top fabric well.

2   Mark on design if using paint or crayon.

3   Spread out backing; place top fabric on it, face uppermost. Tack layers together thoroughly (see page 73).

4   Mark on design if it is being chalked or needlemarked.

5   Stitch round lines of design by hand or machine.

6   Take out tackings.

7   Turn work over.

For small shapes, pull a few threads of the backing aside and insert small pieces of torn off wadding, using a knitting needle or crochet hook to push the filling well into corners and points (figure 46b). Use enough filler to ensure that the shape stands out in relief on the front of the work.

Stroke muslin threads back into place.

46   Inserting the filling for stuffed quilting
(a)   The back of the work with stitching complete
(b)   Parting the threads and pushing in wadding with a knitting needle
(c) and (d)   Alternative method: slitting the backing fabric to insert wadding

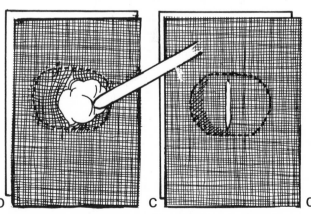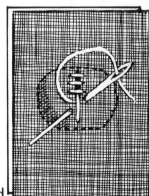

For larger shapes, make a slit in the backing fabric, insert the stuffing and cobble up the slit with a few overcasting stitches (figures 46c and d).

8   All stuffed quilting should be lined.

Stuffed quilting may be combined with wadded quilting in order to emphasise certain portions of the design. The whole process as described above should be carried out on the areas of the design which are to be emphasised, and the prepared fabric then assembled with the wadding and backing for wadded quilting to be carried out in the normal way.

47   *right*   Stuffed shapes with added french knots   Ingrid Rowling

48   *opposite above*   Combination of flat, corded and stuffed quilting Sister Helen McGing

49   *opposite below*   Stuffed quilting worked on a synthetic stretch fabric Ingrid Rowling

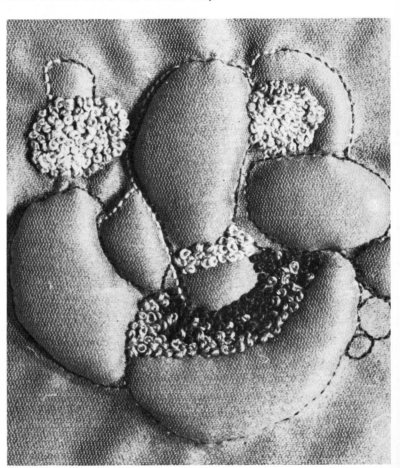

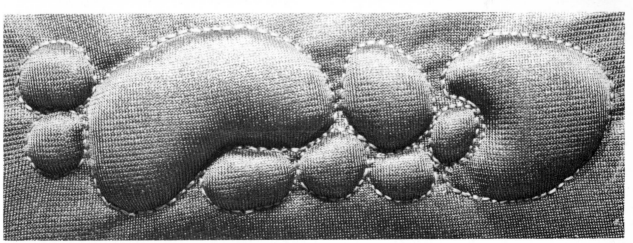

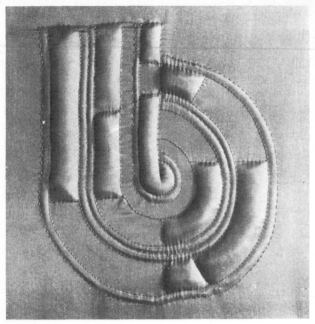

50 *above*   Stuffed and corded quilting
on Jap silk   Celia Goodrick Clark

51 *above right*   Motif in stuffed
quilting   Sister Helen McGing

52 *right*   Free machine embroidery
on velvet with stuffed areas
Sue Jenner

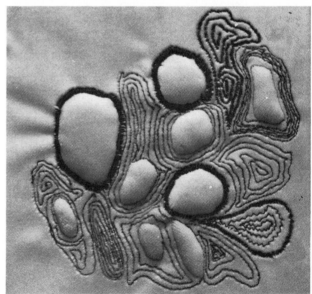

48

shadow quilting

construction	Two layers of transparent fabric with visible filling (figure 53).
purpose	To bring delicacy and colour to what is normally a solid-looking monochromatic medium.
materials	*Top fabric* any transparent fabric such as organdie, voile, muslin, organza, fine silk or lawn.
	Filling embroidery or knitting wools in really strong colours (the colour is toned down considerably when seen through the top fabric), felt, beads, seeds, etc.
	Backing as top fabric.

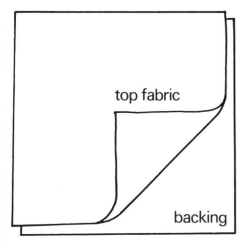

top fabric

backing

53   Construction for shadow quilting:
two layers of transparent fabric

threads	Match to top fabric (ie cotton on cotton, etc).
stitches	*By hand* back stitch.
	By machine straight stitching or free darning.
designs	Designs must consist of enclosed shapes and/or double lines, as in stuffed and corded quilting.

method

(a) For corded and stuffed shadow quilting

1 Iron fabrics.

2 Draw design out full size on paper. Place top fabric over the drawing and trace the lines of the design on with a white pencil or with poster colour and a really fine brush.

3 Put top fabric and backing together, right sides outward and tack thoroughly (see page 73).

4 Carry out stitching by hand or machine.

5 Turn work over. Insert fillings as for normal stuffed or corded quilting, but being careful with the cording not to leave too much of the wool projecting at curves and points or it will show through on to the right side of the work. In enclosed spaces use ends of knitting wool rather than wadding or for a sparkling effect insert beads, making sure that the slit through which they are inserted is sewn up firmly and neatly.

(b) Padding with felt For this type of work the design should consist of simple, flat areas of colour.

1 Lay backing fabric on a table wrong side uppermost. On this arrange felt shapes: do not let them touch each other, always allow enough room for a row or two of stitches in between (figure 54a).

2 Place top fabric right side uppermost over the arranged shapes and tack through all three layers, making sure that a line of tacking passes through each piece of felt (figure 54b).

3 Stitch round the felt shapes in backstitch or by machine.

4 Take out tacking (figure 54c).

54 Shadow quilting. Padding with felt shapes
(a) The felt pieces arranged on the backing
(b) The top fabric in place and all three layers tacked together
(c) The stitching completed and the tacking removed

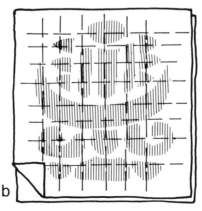
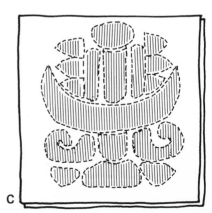

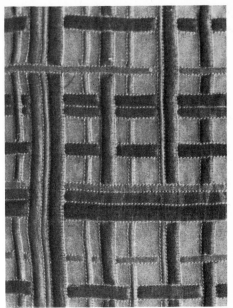

55 *left* Stuffed shapes on white organdie with additional stitching by hand and machine

56 Interlacing lines of corded quilting on white organdie. The lines are threaded with red and orange coloured wools   Sister Helen McGing

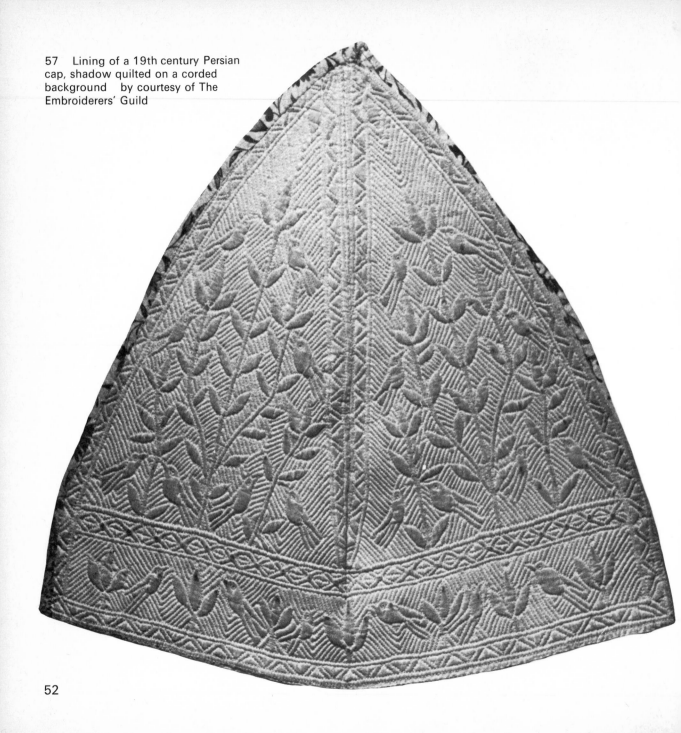

57 Lining of a 19th century Persian cap, shadow quilted on a corded background by courtesy of The Embroiderers' Guild

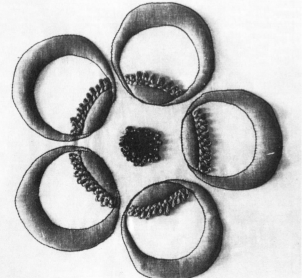

58 *above left* Shadow quilting in organdie over blue felt, with additional hand embroidery
Sister Agnes Bernard

59 *above* Motif in shadow quilting and hand embroidery. Both stuffed and corded quilting are used

60 *left* Shadow quilting worked on the machine with additional hand embroidery Sister Helen McGing

gathered quilting

construction	Two layers of fabric, the top one gathered into a 'ruched' effect (figure 61).
purpose	To give an interesting surface texture.
materials	*Top fabric* this should be fairly stiff; a heavy satin gives a good effect, and even velvet can be used (figure 62). *Backing* same as top.
threads	Match to top fabric (ie cotton on cotton, etc).
design	Areas of gathered quilting must consist of enclosed shapes, but these can be combined with other types of quilting or incorporated into an appliqué design.
method	1 On right side of backing fabric mark the area to be filled with gathered quilting (say a circle) (figure 64a). From top fabric cut a similar shape but twice the size. Turn a small hem on to wrong side and secure with a row of running stitch (figure 64b). When running is complete draw up shape until it is the same size as that marked on to the background fabric. 2 Place it over the marked area and hem in place. 3 At this stage there should be a loose bag standing up from the background (figure 64c). Stab stitch at intervals over the applied patch and the fabric will fall into an interesting surface pattern (figure 64d).

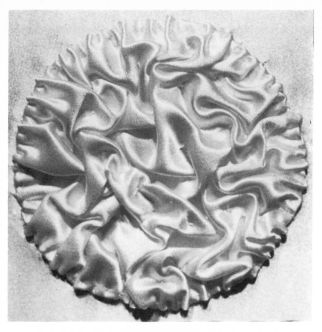

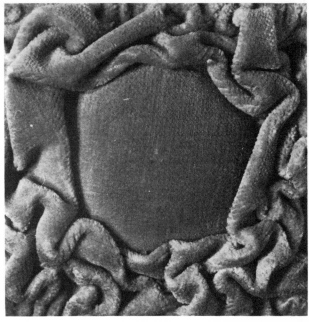

61   *above left*   Gathered quilting

62, 63 *above and left*   Two samples
of gathered quilting on velvet
Ingrid Rowling

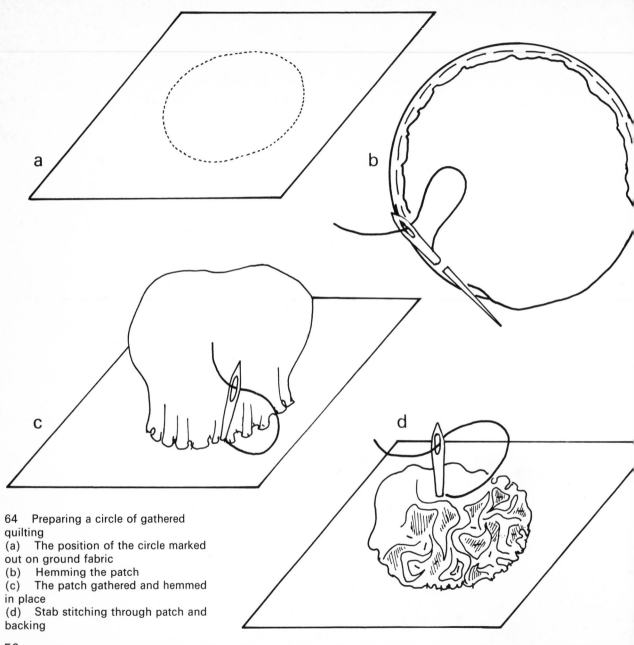

64   Preparing a circle of gathered
quilting
(a)   The position of the circle marked
out on ground fabric
(b)   Hemming the patch
(c)   The patch gathered and hemmed
in place
(d)   Stab stitching through patch and
backing

simulated quilting

Whereas true quilting takes time and patience, there are a number of ways in which a quilted effect can be achieved by quicker means. It must be realised, however, that it is not possible to obtain by these methods the same variety and richness of texture as in real quilting.

pillow quilting

construction Miniature 'pillows' joined together (figure 65e).

purpose To combine patchwork with a quilted effect in one operation.

materials A mixture of colours or patterns and plains in like materials (ie all cottons, all wools, etc).
Filling   pieces of synthetic wadding, foam chips.

threads Ordinary sewing thread for machining, buttonhole twist for over-sewing or a fairly thick embroidery thread such as cotton perlé if faggotting is used to join the pieces.

stitches Straight stitching on the machine. Oversewing or faggotting by hand.

design An arrangement of squares and rectangles.

method 1   Prepare a number of square and/or rectangular pillows in the following way.
For each pillow cut two pieces of fabric the same size, allowing for seams. Place pieces face to face and machine round three sides (figure 65a).
Trim surplus material from corners and turn inside out. Fill with wadding or foam chips (figure 65b) and close opening with slip stitch or neat oversewing (figure 65c).

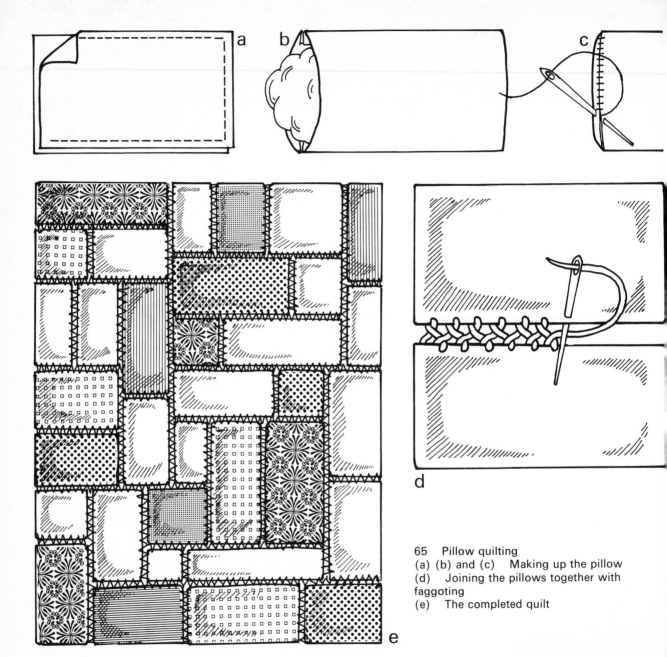

65   Pillow quilting
(a) (b) and (c)   Making up the pillow
(d)   Joining the pillows together with faggoting
(e)   The completed quilt

2 Arrange the prestuffed units to form a pleasing design.

3 Join together with oversewing on the wrong side, or by faggotting for a more decorative effect (figure 65d).

raised patchwork

(also known as Swiss Patchwork).
A variation on pillow quilting, but on a smaller scale and using traditional patchwork shapes.

construction Stuffed geometric patches joined together (figure 67).

purpose To produce an effect of patchwork and quilting in one operation.

materials Closely woven smooth fabrics for the patches. Wadding for filling.

threads Ordinary sewing cotton for machining.
A strong thread such as buttonhole twist for oversewing.

designs Arrangements of geometric units (triangles, hexagons, squares, etc).

method **(a) For triangles**
1 Iron fabric.
2 Cut a number of squares of the same size (use a template for accuracy) (figure 66a).
3 Fold each square in half diagonally, with right side of fabric innermost. Seam up by hand or machine along one side and half way along the other side (figures 66b and c).
4 Trim corners and turn the patch right side out.
5 Stuff patch and close opening with neat oversewing (figures 66d and e).
6 When a number of patches have been prepared they can be arranged in a pleasing design and oversewn together firmly on the back (figure 66f).

(b) For other geometric shapes (eg hexagons) cut *two* pieces of fabric for each patch, lay them face to face and seam up, leaving an opening. Continue as for triangles.

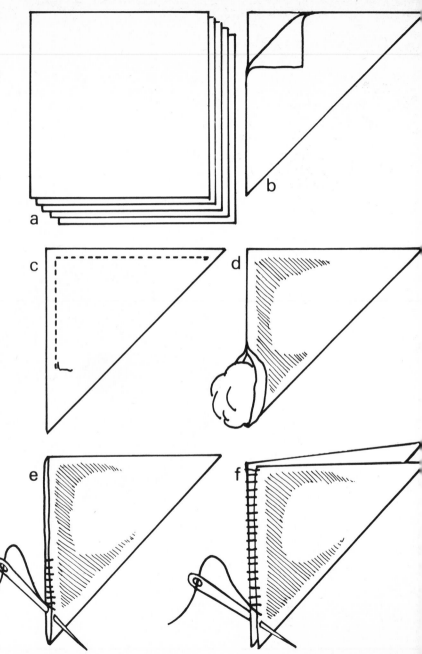

66 *right* Raised patchwork using triangular patches
(a) The patches cut out
(b) A square patch folded and (c) stitched
(d) The wadding inserted
(e) The opening sewn up
(f) The patches oversewn together

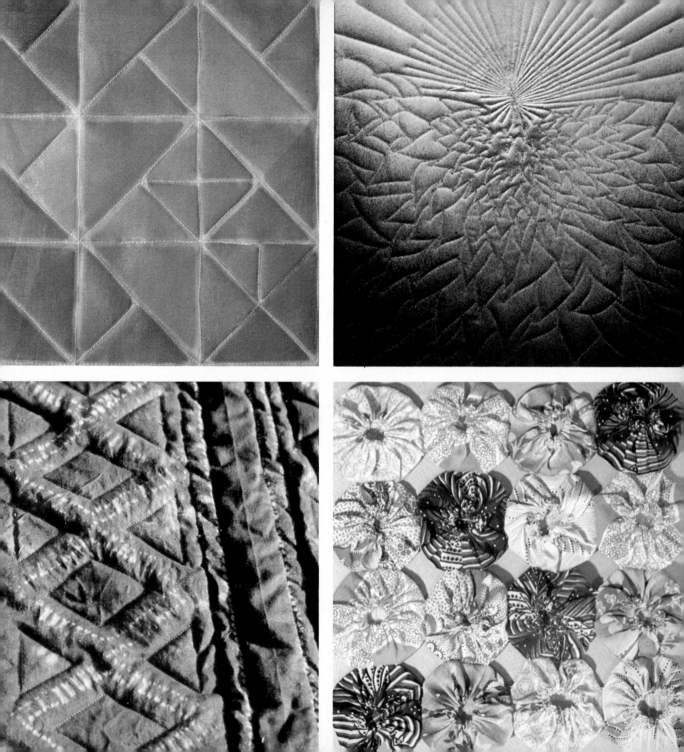

67 *left* Raised patchwork

68 *below* Tonal arrangements of triangular shapes for raised patchwork

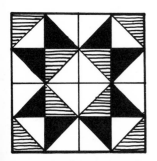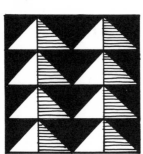

overlapping scales

This is another way of achieving an effect of patchwork and quilting in one operation.

construction Overlapping rows of padded 'scales' stitched to backing, (figure 69).

purpose To simulate patchwork and quilting quickly and easily.

materials An old sheet for backing.
Any closely woven smooth fabric for scales.
Plastic foam sheeting for filling.

threads Match to top fabric (ie cotton on cotton, etc).

designs Arrangements of plain and patterned scales, or scales in varying tones and colours.

method 1 Cut a template of the required size, in card, making the lower edge pointed or curved to choice (figure 70a).
2 Iron fabric, lay on table doubled, face to face.
3 Place template on top and chalk round it (figure 70b).
4 Seam up on chalked line round three sides, leaving the top open. Trim away surplus fabric leaving a little more at top of upper fabric (figure 70c).
5 Turn patch inside out and insert a piece of plastic foam cut exactly to size of template (figure 70d).
6 Turn top fabric over and pin scale to backing (figure 70e).
7 Repeat until there is a row of scales along entire width of backing, at the bottom.
8 Attach to backing with a line of machine stitching near the top of scales (figure 70f).
9 Attach the next row of scales above this, so that the line of stitching is hidden, and so on until the entire backing is covered (figure 70g).

69 Overlapping scales

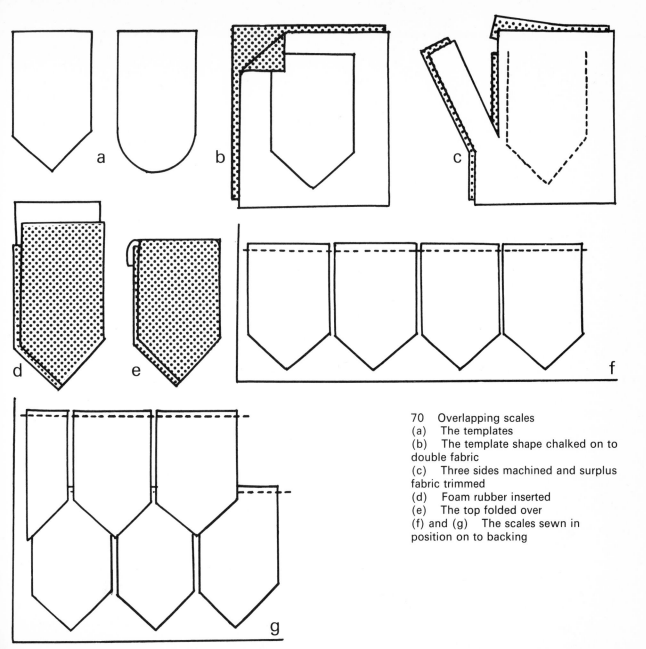

70 Overlapping scales
(a)   The templates
(b)   The template shape chalked on to double fabric
(c)   Three sides machined and surplus fabric trimmed
(d)   Foam rubber inserted
(e)   The top folded over
(f) and (g)   The scales sewn in position on to backing

suffolk puffs or yo-yo quilting

construction Gathered circular patches sewn together (figure 71).

purpose Purely decoration – eg on bedcovers, dress, etc.

materials Fine, closely woven fabrics (cotton or silk) in a mixture of plain colours or prints. Small checks and stripes give interesting results.

threads Strong cotton such as buttonhole twist or a strong silk.

designs Arrangements of circular patches in horizontal and vertical rows.

method 1   Using card, make a round template just over twice the size of the required patch. Cut a number of fabric circles from it, and gather them up as follows.

2   With wrong side of patch facing upwards, turn a narrow hem on to the wrong side and secure with a running stitch (figure 72a).

3   When running is completed draw the patch up tightly and secure thread with a double stitch. Trim thread close to work. Spread gathers evenly and press lightly (figure 72b).

4   Join the patches together, gathered side uppermost, by overcasting with a few stitches on back of work. This slightly squares off the shape of the patch, but it is necessary to give sufficient strength to the resulting fabric. The patches may be joined in a straight repeat or in a half drop (figure 72c).

The joined patches can be mounted on to a backing fabric of contrasting colour, which would show through the holes. This obviously gives greater strength to the work.

71   *opposite*   Suffolk Puffs or Yo-Yos

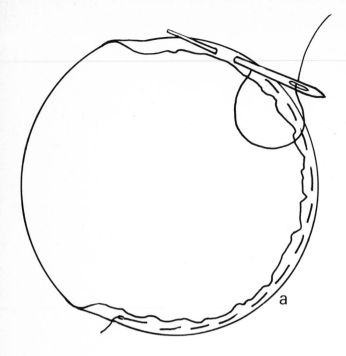

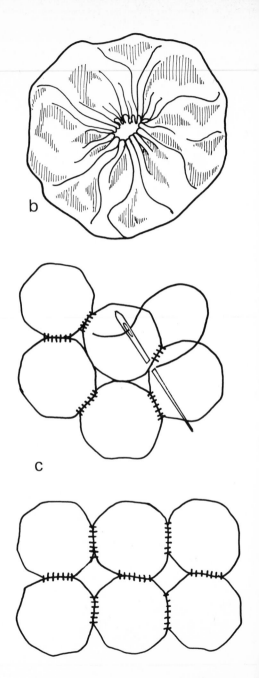

72 Suffolk Puffs
(a) Turning in and gathering the patch
(b) The completed patch, right side
(c) Joining the patches with oversewing

quilted effect with no stitching

Suitable only for panels and rigid constructions such as boxes, mirror frames, etc.

construction Two layers stuck together and with inserted shapes.

purpose To give an appearance of quilting without any stitching.

materials *Top fabric* any closely woven opaque fabric in a *natural* fibre (synthetics will not stand the heat necessary to iron the fabric down to the backing).
Filling cardboard, felt or plastic foam.
Backing iron-on interlining.

designs Simple geometric shapes not too small in scale are the easiest to handle with this method. Place them far enough apart to enable the toe of the iron to pass between them easily.

method 1 Place iron-on interlining sticky side uppermost on table.
2 Arrange cardboard, felt or foam shapes on it (use card for a hard edge effect, felt or foam for softer edges).
3 Place top fabric face uppermost on top and, using the toe of the iron, press close up to the edges of the shapes, until the backing and top fabric are well stuck together (figure 73b).
4 Using the iron flat, press any large spaces in between motifs, making sure that the top fabric and backing are completely fused (figure 73c).

73 *below* Simulated quilting with no stitching
(a) Iron on backing with cardboard shapes in place
(b) Top fabric placed in position
(c) Press close to the edge of the card with the toe of the iron

a

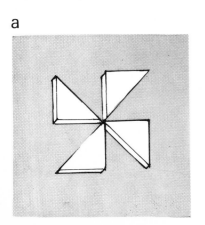

b

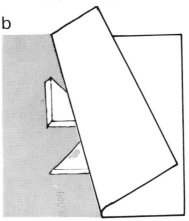

c

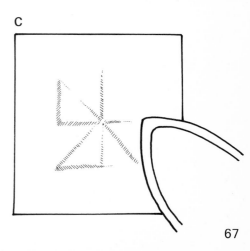

74 Simulated quilting with no stitching

technical hints

equipment

(a)   For quilting by hand

A rectangular frame which consists of two bars with a webbing tape attached (rails) and two flat strips of wood (stretchers). The length of the webbing controls the width of fabric which may be quilted, and the frame is generally sold by this length eg 46 cm (18 in.) tape, 61 cm (24 in.) tape. Frames can usually be bought up to 76 cm (30 in.) tape, but large frames for bed quilts, which are normally 228 cm (90 in.) can be made quite simply to the same pattern.

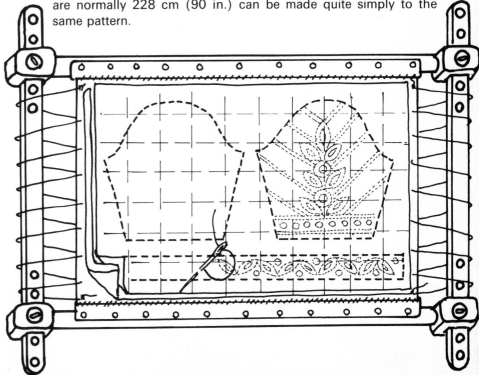

75   Quilting a garment by hand. Pattern pieces are trace tacked on to fabric and the quilting worked before cutting on the garment

Although not always essential, a frame is useful in that it leaves both hands free for the actual stitching – one hand can remain underneath the work to receive the needle as it is pushed through from the top. It also holds the different layers securely in their correct positions.

A round frame for small pieces of work.

Two pairs of scissors; one large pair for cutting out and a small pair (possibly curved) for trimming threads.

Plenty of fine needles; several can be threaded up at once in order to save interrupting the rhythm of the work once it gets going, and they can also be used instead of pins on fabric which marks easily. Thimble.

76, 77   Jacket by Hilary Burns, quilted on a fabric designed and printed by herself

A rug needle for marking designs; a tracing wheel and tailor's chalk for the same purpose.

Templates. These may be metal ones, which can be bought in a variety of shapes and sizes, or card cut to your own design. When making your own template, it is important to measure and cut really accurately.

Stanley knife (craft knife) for cutting card.

(b) For quilting by machine

A quilting foot with gauge; also a raised seam attachment where this is available with the machine.

A round frame for free running.

materials

Where possible it is recommended that fabrics made from natural fibres are used for quilting. This is particularly important where elaborate hand quilting is being contemplated, as most synthetic fabrics are too springy to give the controlled undulating surface which can be obtained with cotton, silk or fine linen. For geometric designs worked on the machine, however, they are practicable and even PVC can, with care, be quilted.

For fillings, on the other hand, the present day synthetic waddings are ideal. In the past a variety of fillings was used including wadding, cotton wool, carded sheep's wool or old blankets, but *Terylene* or *Tricel* wadding have the advantage of being lightweight, washable and quick drying. For less padded quilting, domette is also light and easy to sew through, but is only guaranteed for dry cleaning.

If a dark fabric is being quilted, using a white filling and stitching by hand, the look of the work is sometimes marred by small flecks of the filling being pulled through by the needle. This can be overcome by putting a layer of organdie or muslin immediately

78 *below*   Detail of smock in a mixture of fabrics and delicate colours. Machine quilted with the twin needle at yoke and cuffs, and trimmed with ribbons and swansdown   Rita Delpeche and June Tiley

79 *below right*   Detail of hand quilted dressing gown in eau-de-nil satin and crêpe   Maureen McGrath

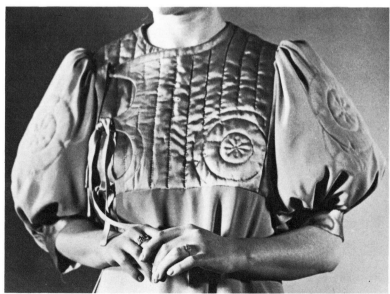

under the top fabric, which will stop the filling pulling through. Alternatively, black domette can be used as a filler.

ironing

Fabrics which are to be quilted should be ironed thoroughly before the layers are tacked together, as it is impossible to get deep creases out after the quilting has been done.

tacking

This should be done from the centre out on small pieces of work and in horizontal and vertical rows on larger pieces (figure 80). It is vital, especially in machine quilting not to skimp on tacking, or the various layers of fabric will move during the working, resulting in unsightly bubbles and wrinkles. The only exception is if a very delicate fabric is being used which would mark badly. In this case it should be possible to pin the layers together with very fine needles until the quilting is completed. This was done with the waistcoat in figure 31.

80 Tacking the layers of fabric together
(a) Out from the centre
(b) In a horizontal and vertical grid

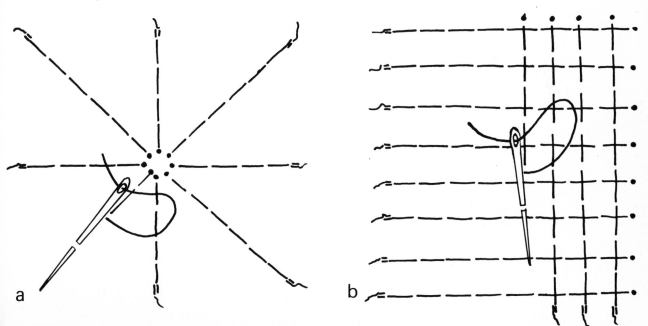

a

b

81　Panel with various techniques, including quilting　Anita-Marie Digby

marking designs

Designs should be marked on the right side of the top fabric by one of the following methods.

(a) *Needlemarking*　This is the cleanest way of putting on the design. It is sometimes called 'scratching' but this is a misnomer as the fabric is never scratched, merely indented. This method is particularly suitable when designs are being built up round templates, or with a ruler. A rug needle is used, never one with a point, as this would damage the surface of the material. It helps to push the needle into a cork, or to thread a length of wool through the eye in order to get a firm grip on the needle while marking. The needle should be held almost parallel with the fabric, with the forefinger outstretched to insert pressure near the tip of the needle, and a clean single indented line made round the template (figure 82c). When using a frame mark only as much as can be reached comfortably, or if the work is being handled as in machine quilting, as much as can be worked in one sitting. Most fabrics which are suitable for quilting will retain an indented line long enough for the stitching to be completed. Synthetics are too springy, and if they are being used are better chalked, although a test should always be made to ensure that the chalk will brush off without leaving a mark. Tailor's chalk should be sharpened to a fine edge, or a well pointed dressmaker's marking pencil may be used, and the drawing done round templates as above. Traditionally, on dark fabrics sharpened dry soap was used.

(b) *Pinging*　Long straight lines can be 'pinged'. Rub a length of string with chalk, and with the help of another person hold it taut immediately above the position of the required line. Pick up the string in the middle and let it go with a sharp 'ping' so that a perfectly accurate straight line is transferred to the fabric.

(c) *Perforating*　The design can be transferred from paper on to the fabric by running over the lines of the design with a tracing wheel (originally a spur was used) (figure 82b). With many fabrics this dotted line will last long enough for the work or a portion of it to be completed, as with needlemarking, but if a more permanent pattern is required a very hard sharp pencil can be used to mark through the holes in the tracing paper, or the design may be pounced and painted. Should the lines of the design be too

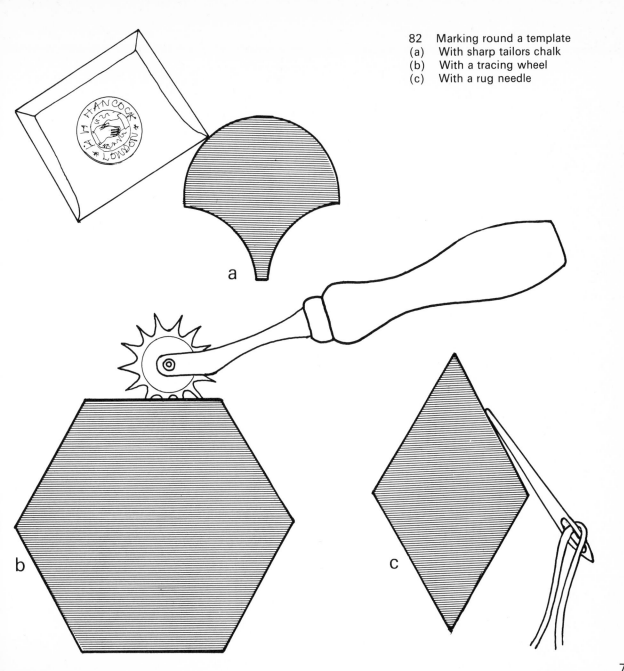

82 Marking round a template
(a) With sharp tailors chalk
(b) With a tracing wheel
(c) With a rug needle

intricate for the use of a tracing wheel a darning needle can be used for the pricking. Perforation can also be done on the machine, with the foot on or as for free running but without a thread. In fact, with a simple machined pattern the actual quilting can be carried out through paper which is then torn away, but this should not be tried with an intricate design.

(d)   Designs can be drawn freehand on the top layer in paint or crayon.

(e)   *Embroidery carbon paper* (sometimes sold as tracing paper) With care, this method can be quite successful. Place the carbon working side down, between the drawing and the fabric, and press through the lines of the design with a fine, hard point. (A ball point pen which has run out of ink is ideal.) Or, run over the design with a tracing wheel. Embroidery carbon is available in a number of colours, for light or dark fabric.

(f)   *Transfers*   Commercial transfers may be ironed on to the

83, 84   Details of two novel bed quilts based on landscapes
83   Cover for a small boy's bed which can be used during the day as a setting for model cars. Made for her son by Barbara Siedlecka

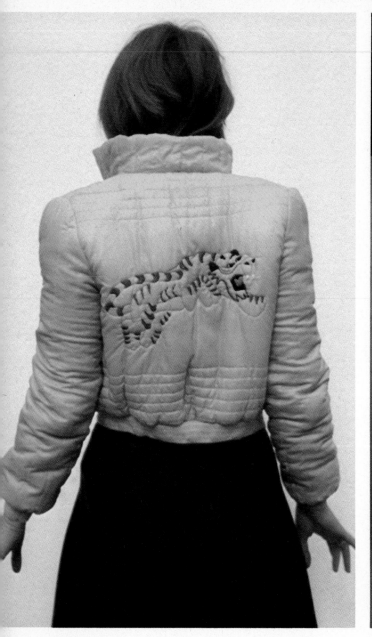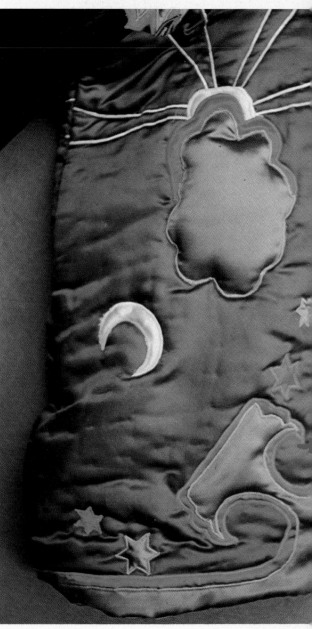

fabric. Banal designs can be made more interesting by cutting up the transfers and moving the pieces around to build up one's own design.

(g) Some traditional quilting, especially in America, was marked by printing with a wood or metal block. As a makeshift, experiments could be made with fabric inks or dyes (available from art shops) on say, pastry cutters, building up patterns as with templates and printing them on to the fabric.

The first three methods should be carried out after the different layers have been tacked together as they are only semi-permanent. The other methods can be done before tacking.

Methods (d), (e) and (f) are not really suitable if the quilting is being done in running stitch as the line will show in the spaces between the stitches. With back stitch, chain stitch or machining the problem does not arise, providing the marked line is kept fine enough.

Plate 8 *opposite left* Jacket with quilted tiger on the back Joy Kleiner

Plate 9 *opposite right* Sleeve, detail of dress with appliqué and quilting Anna-Marie George

84 Rural landscape. The cover is highly padded and all the details such as trees, building and animals made by hand in fabric and thread Susie Pile

stitching by hand

for wadded quilting

To start – bring the needle up on a line of the design 'losing' the knotted end of the thread in the filling. For a really secure start make a small back stitch and go back into it splitting the thread. All stitches are worked from the right side of the work.

(a)   Running   It is essential that the stitch should pierce all

85   Stitches used in hand quilting
(a)   Running
(b)   Back stitch
(c)   Chain stitch
(d)   Pearl effect achieved by working small stitches in thick thread
(e)   Two stages in a true pearl stitch

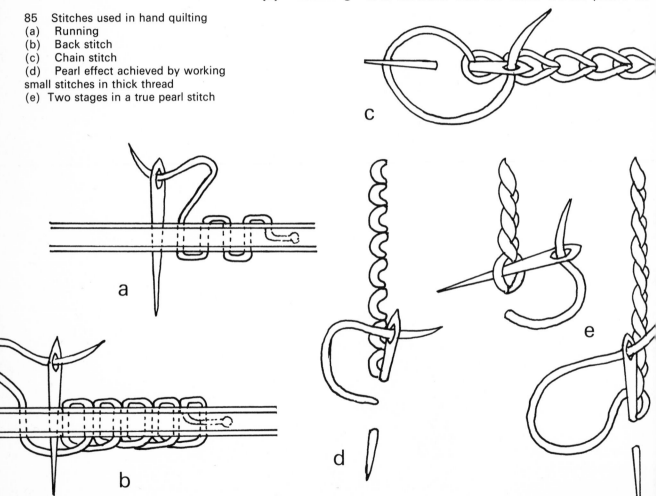

three layers, so for the inexperienced quilter a stab stitch (figure 85a) is recommended. With more experience it is possible to make a run of several stitches before pulling the needle through as in ordinary running. This is done by holding the left hand underneath the work to feel the needle coming through and to guide it back to the surface, while the right hand on top of the work pushes the needle along. This is the method used by professional quilters, but needs a lot of practice to perfect.

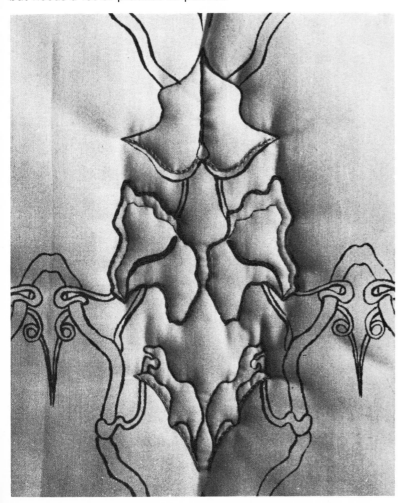

86   Detail of a design. Quilting in back stitch and chain stitch combined with screen printing   Marion Hicks

(b) Back stitch This too is best worked in a stabbing fashion (figure 85b).

(c) Chain When the quilting is held in the hand chain stitch can be worked in one movement (figure 85c), but when the work is in a frame two separate stabbing movements must be made.

(d) 'Pearl' There are two ways of achieving a pearl effect. One is simply to work a very short back stitch in a thick twisted cotton (figure 85d); the other is worked as follows: take a small single stitch, but before drawing it up pass the needle underneath from right to left and then tighten up the stitch. Again, use a thick thread and a short stitch for the best effect (figure 85e).

Finishing off threads: run needle through padding and bring up further along on the marked line. Take needle down over one thread of the material and run through padding again. Repeat until end of thread is used up. The minute stitches on the surface will be completely hidden as the work proceeds.

Stitching by hand for other types of quilting

When stitching flat, corded or stuffed quilting it is not necessary to stab stitch as there is no thick filling to be gone through.

quilting on the machine

Use the quilting foot supplied with the machine. For straight lines and simple repeats insert adjustable gauge into the quilting foot using it to maintain equal distances between lines of stitching (figure 11). This keeps the marking of lines down to a minimum, and adds to the freshness of the work. For non-parallel and more intricate lines remove the gauge to make the work more manoeuverable and the pattern easier to see.

Size of needle depends on the type of fabric used and thickness of work. Heavy padding requires a strong needle. When machining leather or suède insert a special leather needle.

Length of stitch will also depend largely on the scale of the work, but generally speaking a medium length stitch with a slightly loose tension is satisfactory. PVC requires a long stitch, or the perforated fabric tears away like a stamp. PVC sometimes sticks under the foot, and the stitches build up. This can be overcome by putting talcum powder, french chalk or a smear of oil on the top surface before stitching.

87 *opposite* Panel with quilted areas Julia Graham Rogers

88 *above* Child's dungarees in brown, orange and green leather. The quilted pineapple motifs give a hard wearing protection to the knees Maureen Magrath

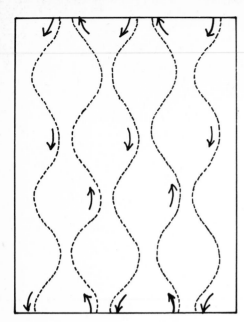

89 Quilting on the machine. Work alternate rows in opposite directions

With wadded quilting, loosen pressure on presser foot and always make sure that the layers are well tacked together. To ensure further that the materials do not ride, hold the work out with the hands on either side of the foot as the stitching proceeds. Stitch alternate lines in opposite directions (figure 89).

As well as straight stitching quilting may be carried out in satin stitch or with set 'automatic' stitches. These could be combined with free stitching to build up geometric filling within shapes, or to give variety of line.

Cable stitch gives a bolder line than ordinary machining and is worked in the following way:

Fill the spool with an unstranded embroidery cotton such as pearl. Loosen the tension screw on the spool case to enable the thread to feed out smoothly. Thread the top of the machine with normal sewing cotton or silk with a slightly tighter tension than usual. Work upside down so that the pearl cotton is on the right side. The stitch has the appearance of a neat couched line. Experiments can be made with length of stitch as this alters the appearance of the stitch considerably.

Free running stitch

This is done with the foot removed and the feed dog lowered, the work being held taut in a round frame when possible. If the quilting is very bulky a frame may be impracticable, but the work can be mounted on vanishing muslin or even held out flat with both hands. This type of work needs practice, but does enable far more intricate work to be carried out on the machine.

Areas of free running may be combined with stitching carried out with the foot on.

Stitching with twin needles gives an effect of cording, and, used in conjunction with the raised seam attachment, gives a true cording (figure 90). Alternatively, tucks can be stitched in the normal way and then threaded with cord.

Large articles in wadded quilting are difficult to manipulate on the machine. It is sometimes possible to roll the spare fabric on the right of the needle tightly, to make the work more manoeuverable, or the quilting could be carried out in blocks and later assembled (see lap quilting, figure 30). Stuffed quilting is ideal for big projects on the machine as all the stitching can be completed before any bulky stuffing is inserted.

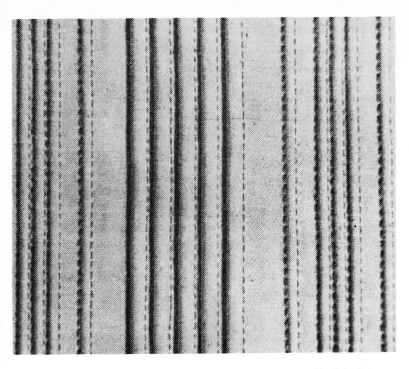

Clean the machine frequently when quilting as fluff builds up quickly round the spool case. Oil regularly for smooth running.

making up a quilted garment

(a)　Using an all over pattern

When the quilting is an all over pattern it is advisable to quilt the entire length of fabric before cutting out the garment. Stitch alternate lines in opposite directions (figure 89) to avoid 'riding' of the layers on each other. If machining use both hands to smooth the fabric outward and away from the foot as the fabric is fed through. Once the entire length of fabric is prepared make up the garment in the usual way but keeping the following points in mind.
(i)　Choose a simple pattern with no gathers or fullness. Sleeves in particular should fit smoothly into the arm-hole. As it is difficult to ease a bulky quilted sleeve into a ready made armhole, leave the sleeve seam and side seam open until after the head of the sleeve

has been set in, and any surplus material can be got rid of in the seam.

(ii)   Do not cut out any of the pattern pieces with the fabric double, even if it is shown thus in the pattern lay out. The bulkiness of the quilted fabric will cause distortion, so cut all pieces opened out.

(iii)   When the pattern pieces are cut and seam lines marked in, remove the filling from the seam allowance by unpicking the quilting and trimming away the wadding. This will make for much neater seams. The same procedure can be used on darts, hems and zip openings.

(iv)   Never turn a double hem in quilted fabric. If the filling is not removed as explained above bind the edge of the fabric and make a single turned up hem.

(b)   Using a quilting pattern designed to the shape of the garment

(i)   Choose a plain fabric. Elaborate quilting can become lost on a busy printed fabric.

(ii)   Plan the design on a paper replica of the dress so that it can be tried on and seen 'in the round'. It is unsatisfactory to plan on a flat surface what will eventually be seen in three dimensions.

(c)   For machined quilting   Cut out all pattern pieces in all three materials – top fabric, filling and backing. Cut them slightly larger than the pattern to allow for shrinkage during the quilting process.

Prepare each piece as for normal wadded quilting, putting the design on the top fabric. Stitch the design only to the seam lines, so that the wadding can be removed easily to make neat seams.

(d)   For hand quilting   Set up work in a frame as for wadded quilting. Trace tack round as many of the pattern pieces as will fit comfortably on to the framed fabric. Mark on the quilting design within these shapes and carry out the stitching, quilting only up to seam lines (figure 66). Remove fabric from frame and cut out pieces. Repeat this procedure until all pattern pieces are prepared. Make up as above.

A garment need not be entirely quilted. Details such as quilted collars, cuffs and pockets may be added to an otherwise plain garment, or quilted sleeves put in for warmth or a quilted hem to add weight to a flimsy fabric.

91 Designs for a collection of quilted
clothes for the daytime David Emanuel

92 *overleaf* Designs for quilted
clothes for the evening David Emanuel

suppliers

Great Britain

Materials and sewing accessories

McCullock & Wallis Limited
25/26 Dering Street
London W1R OBH

for butter muslin, mull, organdie, calico, domette, wadding, iron-on interlining and reasonably priced cotton fabrics, printed and plain. Also piping cord, binding and threads for machine and hand work; needles, pins, scissors, tailor's chalk, marking pencils and tracing wheels

John Lewis & Company Limited
Oxford Street   London W1A 1EX

for a wide selection of fabrics; also beads, interlinings and sewing accessories as above

The Needlewoman Shop
146/148 Regent Street
London W1R 6BA

for linen, quilting muslin, Italian quilting wool, rug wool, a wide range of embroidery cottons; sewing accessories; also templates, round embroidery frames up to 254 mm (10 in.) in diameter and rectangular frames up to a 762 mm (30 in.) tape

Liberty & Company Limited
Regent Street   London W1R 6BA

for a wide selection of fabrics; also suède and leather

Mace and Nairn
89 Crane Street
Salisbury   Wiltshire

for a wide selection of fabrics and sewing accessories

Christine Riley
53 Barclay Street   Stonehaven
Kincardineshire AB3 2AR

for a wide selection of fabrics and sewing accessories; also beads

Limericks
Hamlet Court Road
Westcliff-on-Sea   Essex

for reasonably priced cotton sheeting up to 90 in. wide in white and a good selection of colours

The Felt and Hessian Shop
34 Greville Street   London EC1

for felt in a wide range of strong colours suitable for shadow quilting

Honeywill Limited
Leather Merchants
22a Fouberts Place   London W1

for suède and leather

B & G Leathercloth Limited
71 Fairfax Road   London NW6 4EE

for all types of PVC

Beads

Fred Aldous Limited
The Handicrafts Centre
37 Lever Street
Manchester M60 1UX

Ells & Farrier Limited
5 Princes Street
London W1R 8PH

Sesame Ventures
Greenham Hall
Wellington   Somerset

USA

For a wide variety of materials, threads and accessories

American Thread Corporation
90 Park Avenue   New York

Bucky King Embroideries Unlimited
121 South Drive   Pittsburgh
Pennsylvania 15238

The Needle's Point Studio
7013 Duncraig Court
McLean   Virginia 22101

Yarn Bazaar
Yarncrafts Limited
3146 M Street
North West Washington, DC

Beads

Amar Pearl and Bead Co. Inc
19001 Stringway
Long Island City, NY

Hollander Bead and Novelty
Corporation
25 West 37 Street
New York 18, NY

Leather

Aerolyn Fabrics Inc
380 Broadway   New York

93   Chair cover quilted on the machine by Doreen Nartey. 'Automatic' embroidery stitches have been used